Who eats who in *Rivers* and *Lakes*?

SAINTE DEN STOC

WITHDRAWN FROM
DÚN LAOGHAIRE-RATHDOWN COUNTY
LIBRARY STOCK

Andrew Campbell

W
FRANKLIN WATTS
LONDON·SYDNEY

Designer: Cali Roberts
Editor: Sarah Ridley
Art Director: Peter Scoulding
Editor-in-Chief: John C. Miles
Picture Research: Diana Morris
Artwork: Ian Thompson

© 2005 Franklin Watts

First published in 2005
by Franklin Watts
96 Leonard Street
London
EC2A 4XD

Franklin Watts Australia
Level 17/207 Kent Street,
Sydney
NSW 2000

ISBN 0 7496 6083 X

Dewey classification number: 577.6

A CIP catalogue record for this book is
available from the British Library.

Printed in Malaysia

PICTURE CREDITS

Heather Angel/Natural Visions: 12
Roland Birke/OSF: 16
Martyn Colbeck/OSF: 17
Anthony Cooper/Ecoscene: 15
Reinhard Dirscheri/Ecoscene: 11
Brian Kenny/OSF: 18
Keith Kent/Still Pictures: 10
Gerard Lacz/Still Pictures: 8
Jan-Peter Lahall/Still Pictures: 7
Thomas Mark/OSF: front cover, 1, 25
Chris Martin/Still Pictures: 26
Doug Mazell/OSF: 13
Ted Mead/OSF: 14
Collin Milkins/OSF: 22
OSF: 23
Robert Pickett/Ecoscene: 6, 9
Mike Powles/Still Pictures: 5
Robin Redfern/OSF: 19
Ed Reschke/Still Pictures: 27
Schafer & Hill/Still Pictures: 24
Roland Seitre/Still Pictures: 20, 21
David Woodfall/WWI/Still Pictures: 4

Every attempt has been made to clear copyright.
Should there be any inadvertent omission please apply to
the publisher for rectification.

Note to parents and teachers
Every effort has been made by the Publishers to ensure
that the websites in this book are suitable for children,
that they are of the highest educational value, and that
they contain no inappropriate or offensive material.
However, because of the nature of the Internet, it is
impossible to guarantee that the contents of these sites
will not be altered. We strongly advise that Internet
access is supervised by a responsible adult.

Contents

Who eats who in the water?

A fast-flowing freshwater river

Rivers and lakes are special places for both people and wildlife. They are home to an incredible variety of plants and animals, making them a rich habitat.

Energy and food

All organisms need energy to survive. They get this from their food. Plants can make their own food by capturing energy from sunlight. Animals, however, have to find a food supply within their habitat. For many, this means eating plants. By doing this they take a share of the energy that the plants captured from the sun.

We're in the chain!

Here are some of the river and lake animals that people eat: fish (such as trout, salmon, bass, perch and eel), crayfish, crabs, mussels, oysters and prawns.

Brown trout

What are food chains?

Living things in rivers and lakes are linked to one another by food chains, which are simple lists of who eats what. For example, a leaf falls into a river. An insect nibbles on the leaf before a small fish gobbles up the insect. This small fish then ends up as food for a bigger fish, which an angler eventually catches and cooks. At each link in the chain, energy is passed along from one living thing to another.

Food webs

Food chains in rivers and lakes can be very complicated. With so much life swimming about, many animals do not just eat one type of food, but lots of different types. When food chains get very complex it can be easier to look at them as a food web. A food web shows all the things eaten by animals in one habitat, or place.

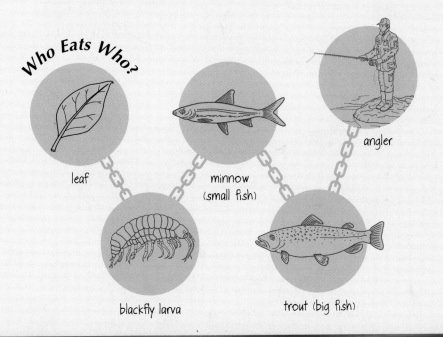

Who Eats Who?

leaf

minnow (small fish)

angler

blackfly larva

trout (big fish)

Yummy!

Cichlids are fish that live in lakes in Africa. Some cichlids eat the scales of other fish. They bump into them and scrape the scales off with their mouths.

Making food

Plants are at the start of most food chains. They are called producers, because they make their energy from sunlight through photosynthesis. This food energy is then passed on to living things higher up the food chain.

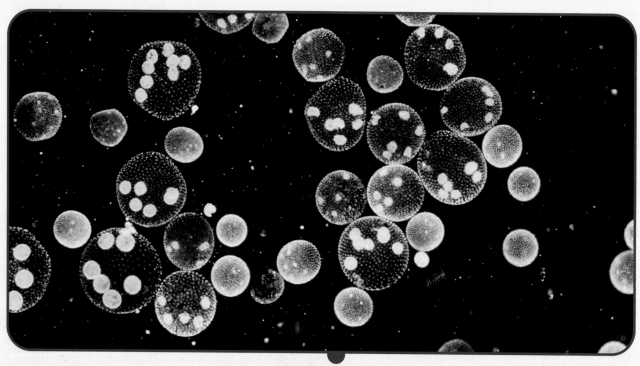

Microscopic algae are the first step in many freshwater food chains.

Small plants

Algae are the most important producers in many rivers and lakes. They are microscopic plants that grow on other plants or rocks, or float in the water. They have different coloured chemicals, called pigments, which help them produce energy from sunlight in different ways. Green algae are very common; other types include golden-brown algae and red algae.

Yummy!

Weevils are a type of beetle. Weevil larvae pierce plants with their tube-like mouths and suck the juice out.

Large plants

Some plants, called emergents, have roots in the soil at the bottom of shallow rivers and lakes, and stems that stick out of the water. They grow like this so that they can capture sunlight to use in photosynthesis. Bulrushes and reeds are emergents and tend to grow at the edge of rivers and lakes. Other plants, like duckweed, float on the surface, while mosses can grow underwater.

Plants from elsewhere

Large plants and algae are like the kitchens of rivers or lakes, making food that feeds many animals. But a lot of the plant material in the freshwater food web comes from elsewhere – like a takeaway meal. Many leaves and branches fall into the water from trees and bushes and are carried along by the running water to feed whoever finds them.

We're in the chain!

People around the world eat watercress, a plant that grows in shallow fast-flowing rivers and streams.

Underwater plants thrive in freshwater lakes.

Along the chain

A great variety of river and lake animals eat plants. They range in size from tiny creatures to snails and fishes.

Grass carp graze on water plants.

Plant-eaters

Plant-eaters are known as herbivores. The smallest herbivores in rivers and lakes are micro-organisms called zooplankton. Zooplankton feed on algae. Bigger animals, such as insect larvae and baby fish, also eat algae. Even some adult fish feed on algae using special filters in their mouths, called gill rakers, which trap the algae like a sieve.

Yummy!

Grass carp do not have teeth, but pieces of bone line the passage from their mouth to their stomach. These bones break up the plants that the fish swallow.

Who Eats Who?

water lily

water snail

jacana (bird)

Grass carp

Bigger water animals may also eat larger plants. One type of animal that likes to eat larger plants is the water snail. Another is a fish called the grass carp, which originally comes from China and can grow to more than a metre long. If there are too many large plants in a river or lake, people sometimes put grass carp in the water to eat them up.

Meat-eaters

Animals that eat herbivores are called carnivores (meat-eaters). Carnivores in rivers and lakes come in all different sizes, from more types of zooplankton to large fish and birds. But many creatures that live in the water are omnivores – they eat plants and animals. Some animals are accidental omnivores, like the grass carp. It may swallow small animals that live on the plants it eats. Other animals like to vary their diets.

A water snail munches on a plant stem.

Hunters

Rivers and lakes can be dangerous places for the creatures that live in them. There are many hunters in the water, but for each one there is often a bigger hunter, on the lookout for a meal.

Small but deadly

Many small and medium-sized animals in the water are fierce hunters. These animals include fishes and insect larvae. Dragonfly larvae can quickly shoot out a part of their mouth, like an arm, to catch their prey. This part of the mouth, called a labrum, has two teeth at the end, which bite into the victim.

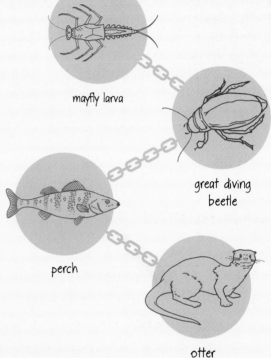

Who Eats Who?

algae

mayfly larva

great diving beetle

perch

otter

Dragonfly larvae are fierce hunters.

Pike are skilled hunters, feeding on smaller fish.

Top hunters

The top hunters in rivers and lakes eat the smaller hunters. They are at the top of food chains, so there is nothing else that will eat them. One top hunter is the pike, a large fish (up to 120 cm in length) with a long head and strong, sharp teeth. Another top hunter is the otter, a shy animal that lives along riverbanks and swims in the water. Otters' long whiskers help them detect movements made in the water by creatures they like to eat, such as fish, crayfish and frogs.

Yummy!

The giant water bug kills its prey by injecting a poison that turns the prey's insides to liquid. The water bug then sucks the liquid up as food.

Different tactics

Some hunters sit and wait for a meal to come along. The pike, for example, hides among plants at the edge of rivers and lakes before pouncing on smaller fish. Other hunters are much more active. The great diving beetle traps bubbles of air under its wings. It then dives under the water and, like a scuba diver, uses the stored air to breathe. It spends a long time looking for the animals it likes to eat, such as mayfly larvae.

Fast-flowing water

Fast-flowing streams and rivers in hilly, wooded areas have food chains all of their own. The water may be too rapid for large plants or microscopic algae to grow, so the first source of food is often fallen leaves.

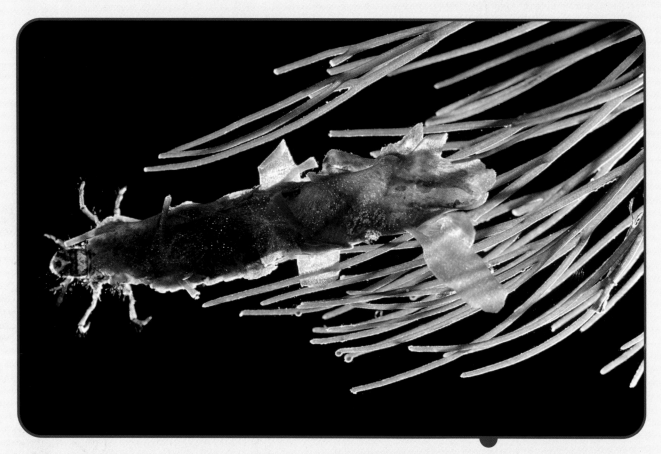

The caddisfly larva – a collector – builds itself a protective case from small stones and shredded leaves.

Shredders

Once leaves have fallen in the water the first thing to eat them is a type of fungi called *hypomycete*. The spores (cells) of the fungi stick to the leaves as they break them down. The next creatures to eat the leaves eat the spores, too, which actually makes the leaves taste better, like a filling in a sandwich. These creatures, such as stonefly larvae, are called shredders because they shred the leaves up with their sharp jaws.

Collectors

The shredders then pass the leaves out, in much smaller pieces, as waste, which falls to the bottom of the river. This becomes food for animals known as collectors. Some collectors, like snails and limpets, scrape this waste off the bottom. Other collectors, like freshwater prawns, use fine hairs on the end of their legs to pick up the bits of leaf and eat them.

Fish food

The churning waters of fast-flowing streams and rivers are full of oxygen, as well as shredders and collectors. They are ideal sites for many fish to spawn (lay eggs). Fish such as salmon and trout can swim thousands of kilometres from the sea back to these streams to spawn (see pages 24-25). Their young, called fry, feed on the shredders.

Yummy!

As well as tiny leaf particles, up to half the collectors' diet is made up of the shredders' poo!

The water in this fast-flowing stream is full of oxygen.

Slowing down

As a river flows towards the sea it becomes wider and slows down. Different plants and animals live in it now; many of them also live in the shallow parts of lakes.

Sediment

The remains of dead leaves and dead animals from upstream flow down and settle on the bottom of slow-moving rivers and lakes. They form layers of sand and mud, called sediment. This sediment, as well as the slower movement of the water, provides good living conditions for many fish, such as bass and perch, as well as freshwater prawns, crabs and crayfish.

Still water provides ideal conditions in which water lilies can grow.

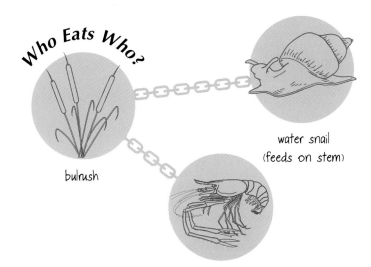

Who Eats Who?

bulrush

water snail
(feeds on stem)

freshwater prawn
(feeds on algae growing on stem)

We're in the chain!

People eat fish eggs, too – especially the eggs of the sturgeon fish. These eggs are called caviar, and are very expensive to buy.

Plants at the edge

The edge of slow-moving rivers and lakes is also home to many large plants that take root in the sediment. Some animals, like water snails, graze on plants like reeds and water-lilies. Other creatures feed on the algae that cling to the plant stems. These feeders include prawns and insect larvae.

Fish, frogs and newts

Bass and perch lurk among the plants on the edge of rivers and lakes, on the lookout for smaller fish to eat. Other animals that hunt here are frogs and newts. These animals are amphibians – they can live in and out of the water. Both fish and amphibians lay eggs in the shallow parts of rivers and lakes.

A frog perches on top if its eggs, or frogspawn.

Out on the lake

Out in the middle of a big lake, things can be very different from a river or stream. The water is deeper and colder, and there may not be any visible plants.

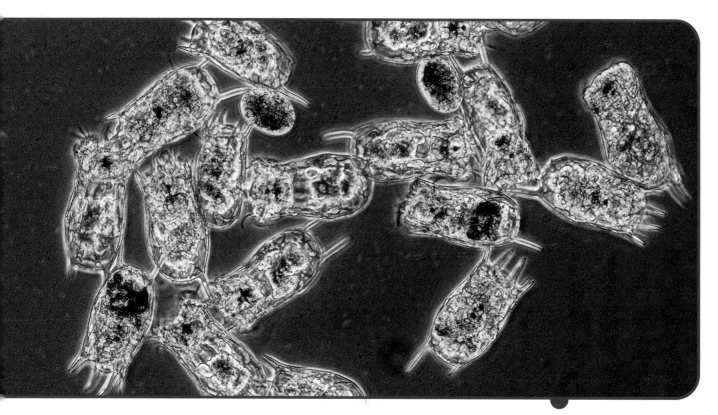

These tiny rotifers are about half the size of a full stop on this page.

Micro-chains

But lake water contains millions of micro-organisms in every litre. These include algae, bacteria and zooplankton. Tiny food chains link these organisms. Bacteria, for example, absorb nutrients from dead plants and animal waste. Next, tiny creatures called protozoans eat the bacteria. Then bigger animals, like rotifers, eat the protozoans.

We're in the chain!

Many bacteria in lakes and rivers get into our water supply – and into us! Usually, the bacteria in our water are quite harmless.

Bigger chains

These micro-chains create food for bigger animals, like prawns and fish. In turn, these feeders are eaten by other fish. In Lake Chad in Africa, for example, micro-chains are at the start of bigger food chains. A prawn may eat small zooplankton; the ferocious tiger fish then snaps the prawn up. But the tiger fish is the favourite food of a much bigger fish, the Nile perch, which can grow to the size of an adult human.

Yummy!

The North American walleye fish's favourite meal is the yellow perch. But the walleye must swallow it head first, otherwise its spiny fins get stuck in the walleye's throat.

Eagles and seals

Yet big fish are not always at the top of the food chain in lakes. On Lake Superior in the USA, one of the top hunters is the bald eagle, which plucks fish out of the water with its sharp talons (claws). One of the largest hunters in Lake Baikal in Russia is a very different sort of animal. This is the Baikal seal, the only seal in the world that lives in fresh water.

Baikal seals

17

On the edge

The banks of rivers and the shores of lakes are important places for many plants and animals, providing water, shelter and, for some animals, other creatures to hunt.

We're in the chain!

The bark of the willow tree, which grows by rivers and lakes, is used to make aspirin – a medicine that helps relieve both headaches and heart problems.

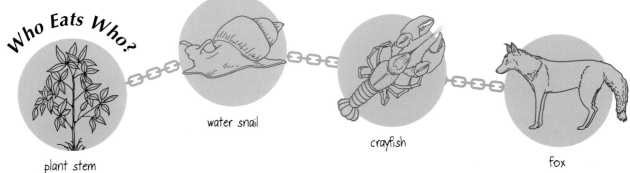

Who Eats Who?

plant stem

water snail

crayfish

fox

Foxes can scoop crayfish out of the water with their paws to make a tasty meal.

18

Yummy!

Water voles like to eat their food near the water's edge. River experts can tell when a water vole has been feeding because it will leave chewed plant stems behind.

Water vole

Trees and birds

Grasses, shrubs and trees grow well in the damp, rich soils by the edge of rivers and lakes. Trees such as alders, maples and willows commonly grow alongside rivers. Birds like wagtails and thrushes make their nests in these trees. They feed on seeds and berries, as well as on insect larvae in the water and adult insects flying above it.

Wetland plants

Some water plants spread from the shallow parts of rivers to form wetlands. In spring, when there are heavy rains and rivers burst their banks, these wetlands fill with water. Amazingly, some wetland plants are carnivores. The pitcher plant, for example, catches insects in its cup-shaped leaves, which are full of water. The insect drowns and the plant absorbs nutrients from it once it has broken down.

Living on the edge

Many animals come to the edge of rivers and lakes to drink and feed. Foxes and deer come to the water's edge, especially in winter when water is frozen elsewhere. Other animals, such as water voles and beavers, live in burrows on river banks or lake shores. Both these animals are herbivores. Water voles feed mostly on grasses, while beavers' favourite food is tree bark.

At the bottom

The bottom of a river or lake may be dark and murky, but it is full of life. Many animals live and feed on the bottom, among rocks, mud or sand.

We're in the chain!

Blackfly and midge larvae live on the bottom of rivers and lakes. As adults, these insects feed off animal and human blood.

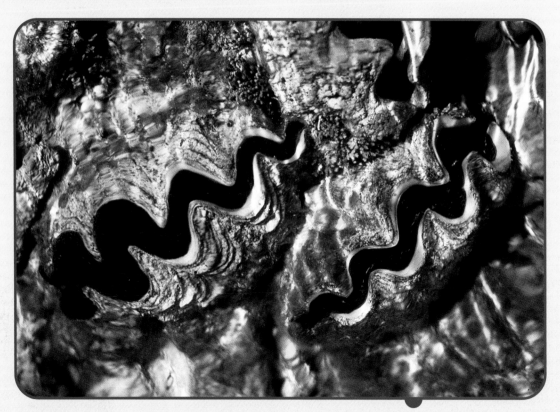

Freshwater clams

Decomposers

At the bottom of slow-moving rivers and lakes there is often a layer of sand or mud deeper than the length of your finger. This sediment is home to different types of insect larvae, as well as shellfish such as clams and mussels.

Many of these animals are decomposers. They eat dead plants and animal waste, such as old fish scales, that have sunk to the bottom. When this dead matter passes through them it is broken down into smaller and smaller pieces.

Who Eats Who?

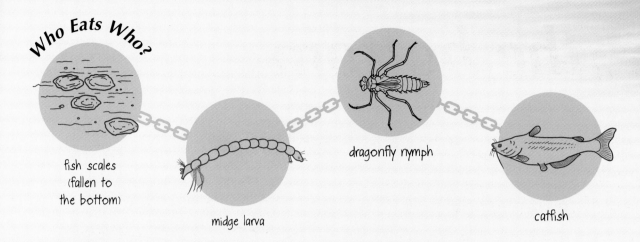

fish scales (fallen to the bottom)

midge larva

dragonfly nymph

catfish

Catfish

Some fish, such as catfish, spend most of their lives on the bottom of rivers and lakes. Catfish range in size from 4 cm to 4.5 m. They get their name from their long feelers, which look like a cat's whiskers. Catfish are decomposers, but they are also omnivores, eating insect larvae. Bigger catfish hunt at night for fish, frogs and even water birds.

Travelling feeders

Some animals live on the bottom during the day but swim up to the surface to feed at night. Water fleas swim up from the sediment to eat zooplankton in the waters above. They feed when it is dark to avoid being eaten by fish, which need the daylight to see the tiny fleas.

A catfish

On the surface

On the surface of rivers and lakes there is a film, or skin, where the water meets the air. This skin is called the surface tension, and is a hunting ground for many creatures.

Yummy!

A water boatman digs its needle-like mouthpart, called a rostrum, into its victim, before sucking out all the body juices.

Rowing insect

The water boatman is an expert water surface hunter. This flat, boat-shaped insect uses its back legs like a pair of oars to row across the water. It feeds on flying insects that have become trapped in the surface tension – caught half in and half out of the water. The water boatman senses the desperate movements, moves in and grabs the insect with its front and middle legs, and spears it with its mouth.

A water boatman searches for prey.

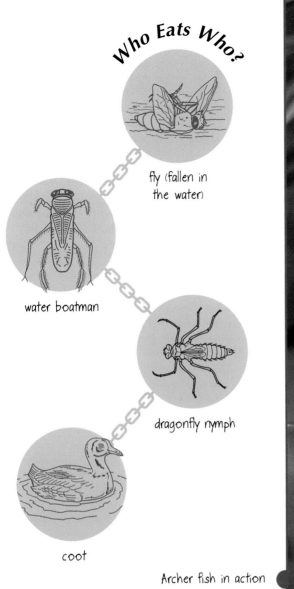

Who Eats Who?

fly (fallen in the water)

water boatman

dragonfly nymph

coot

Archer fish in action

Spitting fish

Fish often break the surface tension to feed on floating or flying insects. Like other types of fish, the black-striped archer fish can jump out of the water to catch flies. But the archer fish has another way of hunting insects above the water. From its mouth, it spits a jet of water at an insect. The stunned insect falls into the water, and the archer fish gobbles it up.

Swimming birds

Ducks and dippers are birds that spend most of their lives swimming on the surface of rivers and lakes. You may have seen ducks raise their bottoms in the air as they put their heads underwater. This is because they are looking for food, such as insect larvae. Dippers dive more deeply than ducks. They use their wings like flippers, swimming to the bottom in search of fish and shellfish.

Salmon food chains

Some animals belong to different food chains at different times in their lives. Salmon are an amazing example: they can swim thousands of kilometres from rivers to the sea, and then back again.

Growing up

Baby salmon (fry) hatch in April or May in fast-flowing rivers and streams. For the first six weeks they feed on the egg yolk that surrounded them before they hatched. Then the fry start to hunt insect larvae. After a year or more, the young salmon swim downstream to where the river meets the sea. Here they eat small fish, prawns and crayfish. Eventually they swim out to sea.

Spawning adult salmon

Yummy!

During their time at sea, salmon eat small fish such as herring and sprats, as well as shrimps.

Coming home

After up to four years at sea, the salmon swim back to the same river where they were born. They are fat from all the food they have eaten in the sea, but they use up all this energy on their journey, which can be thousands of kilometres long and involve jumping many waterfalls. Once the females have spawned and the males have fertilised the eggs, many salmon are so tired that they die. Their dead bodies become food for other animals.

We're in the chain!

Salmon is a favourite food for many people. Much of the salmon sold by shops is farmed, but some is caught at sea, or in rivers for sport.

Salmon hunters

Salmon do not eat much on their long journeys upstream, but they may snap at flies on the surface of the water. Anglers use hooks with artificial flies on the end to fool salmon into snapping at them – the salmon's mouth then catches on the hook. Another salmon hunter is the huge grizzly bear, which grabs the fish as they leap out of the water to jump up a waterfall.

Alaskan grizzly bears stand in waterfalls to catch salmon as they leap upstream.

Rivers, lakes and people

We're in the chain!

Dangerous chemicals can get into rivers and lakes from farms, factories or even from our own homes. These chemicals then get into food chains, where they can poison animals.

Many people around the world depend on freshwater fishing for their livelihoods.

There are many freshwater food chains to which we belong – either because we are consumers, at the top of the chain, or because our actions affect the rest of the chain.

Fishing

Salmon, trout, crayfish and crabs are all river and lake animals that people love to eat, as well as to catch. Fishing is a very popular sport around the world. But catching too many animals means that others in the food chain, such as otters and fish-eating birds, may starve. One way to prevent this is to limit the number of fish people can catch.

Unwanted passenger

We can affect freshwater food chains in other ways, too. For example, in the 1980s, ships from Europe took an unwanted passenger to the USA. This was the zebra mussel. Today, zebra mussels dominate many rivers and lakes in the USA. They eat huge amounts of algae, so there is little left to feed the native American mussel or zooplankton.

Managing food chains

The good news is that the more we know about food chains, the more we can protect them. For example, too many blue-green algae can be harmful because they block out sunlight and oxygen from the water. But if we increase the number of large fish that eat smaller, zooplankton-eating fish, then there will be more zooplankton to eat up the algae and so reduce its numbers. This will lead to an improvement in water quality.

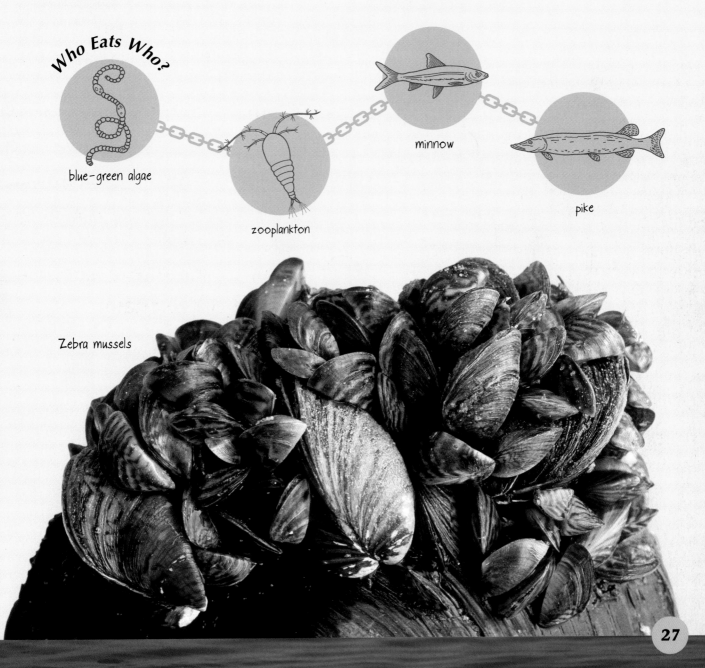

Who Eats Who?

blue-green algae

zooplankton

minnow

pike

Zebra mussels

Freshwater food web

Here is a freshwater rivers and lakes food web. Surrounding it are some fascinating watery facts.

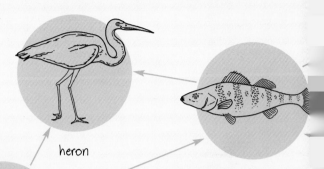
heron

perch

minnow

Female fish called bitterlings grow long tubes through which they lay their eggs in freshwater mussels – the mussel's hard shell protects the fish's eggs.

dragonfly nymph

water snail

caddisfly larva

water flea

bulrush

Giant South American water lilies can be up to 1.2 m wide, and strong enough to support the weight of a child!

Many insects die when it gets cold, but their young (larvae) survive by burying themselves in the mud.

algae

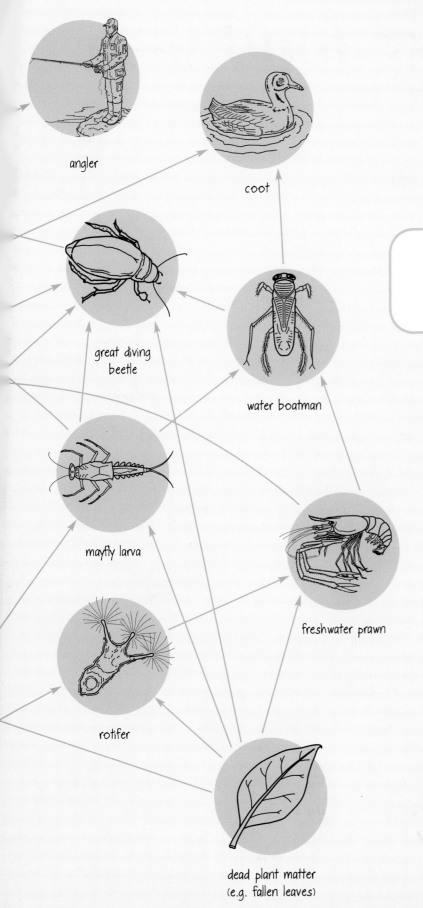

angler

coot

great diving beetle

water boatman

mayfly larva

freshwater prawn

rotifer

dead plant matter
(e.g. fallen leaves)

Mosquito larvae hang upside down in slow-moving waters. They breathe in oxygen through their tails.

Giant otters can grow up to 1.4 m in length – possibly longer than you!

Dippers are able to walk underwater in fast-flowing streams and rivers, hunting for insects.

Female sockeye salmon can lay more than 4,000 eggs.

People sometimes make rivers straighter or deeper to prevent floods – but this can have bad effects on food chains.

Glossary

alga (pl. algae)
a very simple type of plant that does not have stems, roots or leaves.

angler
a person who catches fish, either with a hook and a rod, or with a net.

bacterium (pl. bacteria)
a tiny, one-celled micro-organism that lives in water, as well as in soil, plants and animals' bodies.

carnivore
a meat-eating animal.

collector
an insect larva or other small animal that gathers and feeds on very small pieces of plant food, like leaf parts, in the water.

consumer
a living thing that feeds on another living thing.

decomposer
a living thing that feeds on and breaks down dead plants and animals, as well as animal waste.

emergent
a plant with roots that grow in the soil underwater, and a stem that sticks out above the water.

fresh water
water that runs in rivers and streams, or in lakes that are fed by rivers. Fresh water is different to salt water in seas, or stagnant (still) water in some ponds and swamps.

fry
a baby fish that hatches from an egg.

fungus (pl. fungi)
a flowerless plant that lives on dead or rotting things. Mould, mushrooms and rust are all types of fungus.

habitat
the place where particular living things usually live, and which provides everything they need to survive.

herbivore
a plant-eating animal.

larva (pl. larvae)
a baby insect that hatches from an egg and looks like a small worm. A caterpillar is a type of larva.

micro-organism

a tiny living thing only visible with the use of a microscope. Bacteria, zooplankton and some algae are all micro-organisms.

mouthpart

part of an insect's mouth that sticks out and is used for feeding.

omnivore

an animal that eats plants and other animals.

organism

any living thing, including plants, animals and bacteria.

oxygen

a substance found in air and water, which all living things need to breathe.

photosynthesis

the process by which plants capture the energy of sunlight to make food for themselves.

producer

a living thing that produces its own energy. Plants are producers.

protozoan

a tiny single-celled animal.

sediment

material in liquid form that settles at the bottom. In rivers and lakes, sediment contains dead plant and animal material.

shredder

insect or other animal with strong, sharp mouthparts that allow it to shred and chew plant material.

wetland

a place that forms a link between land and water. It may be covered in water all the time, or only after flooding.

Rivers and lakes websites

http://octopus.gma.org/streams/life.html
A clear guide to life and food chains in streams and rivers.

http://waterontheweb.org/under/lakeecology/
Lots of detailed information and diagrams about plant and animal life in lakes.

http://www.bbc.co.uk/nature/animals/wildbritain/habitats/freshwater/index.shtml
This BBC site has lots of facts and pictures about freshwater habitats, including rivers, lakes, ponds and wetlands.

Index